Passage between Rivers

Passage between Rivers:

A Portfolio of Photographs with a History
of
The Delaware and Raritan Canal

By
Elizabeth G. C. Menzies

Rutgers University Press
New Brunswick, New Jersey

Library of Congress Cataloging in Publication Data

Menzies, Elizabeth G C
    Passage between rivers.

    1. Delaware and Raritan Canal—Pictorial Works.
2. Canals—New Jersey—History.   I. Title.
HE396. D3M46   385 .48'0974941   76-40291

ISBN   0–8135–0831–2 (Cloth)
ISBN   0–8135–0832–0 (Paper)

First Printing

To Auntie Lottie,
my oldest friend

PREFACE

The Delaware and Raritan Canal achieved a position of national importance in its heyday. It not only conveyed cargoes from the flanking states of Pennsylvania and New York, it also was a link between New England and the South, carrying supplies during the Civil War and even moving gunboats through its channel. That eminent authority Wheaton J. Lane (*From Indian Trail to Iron Horse*) has said, "The national significance of the Delaware and Raritan can be seen from the great volume of through traffic which it carried. . . . there were years in which it surpassed in tonnage such a great waterway as the Erie."

I have refrained from listing tonnages, company directors, and dollar sums. Nor have I discussed the political clout of the Joint Companies and the anonymous accusations, in 1848, by Henry C. Carey in the *Burlington Gazette*. Whether there were two sets of book, one used by the officers of the companies in paying dividends and another with the real and greater figures, is still open to question.

The small illustrations opposite the text are supplemented by my own photographs.

The canal has gained a new importance since those early days, when the rolling black smoke of factory chimneys was thought to depict progress. Today it makes a welcome ribbon of green across the ever increasing congestion of central New Jersey.

The Canal and Its Surrounding Area

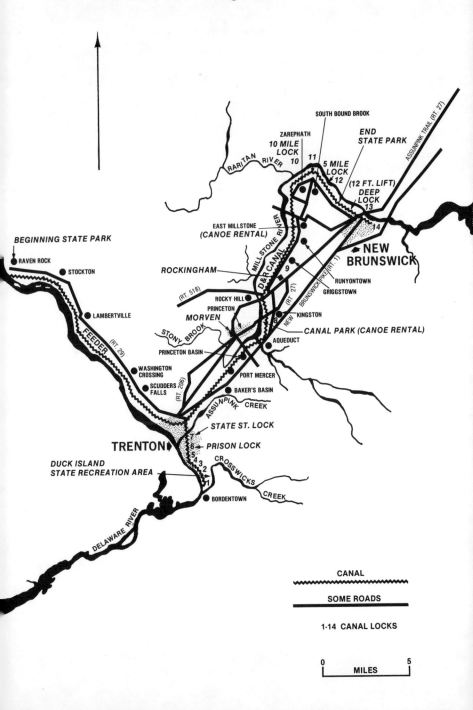

SOUTH BOUND BROOK

ZAREPHATH

END STATE PARK

10 MILE LOCK
10

11

5 MILE LOCK
12

ASSUNPINK TRAIL (RT. 27)

RARITAN RIVER

(12 FT. LIFT)
DEEP LOCK
13

14

EAST MILLSTONE (CANOE RENTAL)

MILLSTONE RIVER

D&R CANAL

NEW BRUNSWICK

BEGINNING STATE PARK

RAVEN ROCK

STOCKTON

ROCKINGHAM

9

RUNYONTOWN

BRUNSWICK PIKE (RT. 1)

GRIGGSTOWN

(RT. 518)

ROCKY HILL

PRINCETON

LAMBERTVILLE

FEEDER (RT. 29)

MORVEN

STONY BROOK

(RT. 27)

8

NEW

KINGSTON

CANAL PARK (CANOE RENTAL)

PRINCETON BASIN

AQUEDUCT

WASHINGTON CROSSING

SCUDDERS FALLS

(RT. 206)

PORT MERCER

BAKER'S BASIN

ASSUNPINK CREEK

STATE ST. LOCK

TRENTON

7 6
5
4 3 2
1

PRISON LOCK

CROSSWICKS

DUCK ISLAND STATE RECREATION AREA

BORDENTOWN

CREEK

DELAWARE RIVER

〰〰〰〰〰 CANAL

───── SOME ROADS

1-14 CANAL LOCKS

0   5
├────────┤
MILES

The canal near Kingston. (Print made from a positive color slide)

The Delaware and Raritan Canal was at last begun in 1831. William Penn and his West Jersey Proprietors had projected a canal across the waist of New Jersey in 1676. To their Commissioners in the Province they wrote, "for Wee intend to have a way cut Cross ye Country to Sandy Hook soe ye further up the River Delaware y^t way will be the Shorter in."

The country had not yet been surveyed, and the inadequate 1675 Sellar map, drawn for East Jersey Proprietor Sir George Carteret, shows north where we place east, and gave "New Jarsey" the figure of a waistless fat lady reclining on her side. The country was not ready for a canal.

Quaker William Penn
as a soldier in Ireland
in 1666.

(Reproduction of an
engraving of the
painting)

Map
by John Sellar copied, by and large, from maps by Nicholas
Joan: Visscher and Augustin Herrman. (From the collections of
the New Jersey Historical Society)

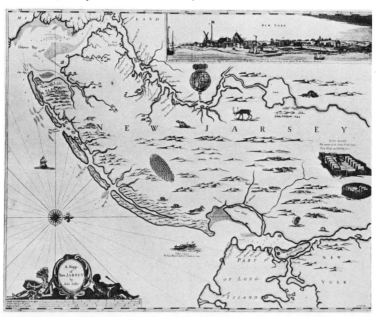

Spiles in the canal at the railway bridge, Princeton

Plans for a canal lay dormant for over a hundred years during which private enterprise helped in the building of roads across the waist of New Jersey. The Indian Assunpink Trail, between the two great rivers and once travelled by New Netherlanders, was improved under British rule. Today we call the trail Routes 27-206.

Before 1686, John Inians, an innkeeper applying for ferry rights at New Brunswick (Inians' Ferry), cleared and cut six miles from the road. By his own account, the work put him "at a Considerable Expence to accomodate the Country," a cost which he no doubt redeemed through road tolls, ferry fees, and his improved inn business.

NEW OMNIBUS

Nineteenth-century engravings

At Little Rocky Hill, where the old road winds away from the early twentieth-century straightened version (Route 27)

Inians' road was called the Upper Road, the Old Road, the Great Highway, the King's Highway, the York Road (to New York), Main Street at Kingston, and Nassau Street in Princeton. These two villages stood at the half-way point between the Delaware and Raritan rivers and between the developing cities of New York and Philadelphia.

Though by the eighteenth century innkeepers were taxed so that government road commissioners could maintain the roads, innkeeping expanded in the two mid-point villages.

The first stage wagon on the route was advertised in 1738. It ran twice a week and was equipped, as one traveller remarked, "with Benches, and Cover'd over, so that passengers may sit Easy and Dry. . . ."

Nineteenth-century egg-shaped stagecoach

Jugtown on what was once the Indian Assunpink Trail. This is now part of Princeton. (Picture taken in the 1970s)

By 1776, the armies of the Revolution were tramping the roads between the two rivers. On January 3, 1777, General Washington took Princeton. He then retired by the Great Highway (Route 27) to Kingston, where he turned along the road to Rocky Hill (by the Kingston Churchyard). He continued to Griggstown, where he crossed the Millstone River by the causeway there, before pausing at the Van Doren house in Millstone.

The Van Doren house, Millstone, in 1966

Map of early roads related to the Battle of Princeton. Washington took the route down the Millstone River, where the canal was later built

The Griggstown Causeway and the old quarters for the canal's mule drivers. (Picture taken in 1975)

Staging made innkeeping into a prosperous business. At Kingston, Phineas Withington could count at one time forty-nine stages and some four hundred harnessed horses standing at his inn. John Joline of the Nassau Hotel (later the Nassau Inn) at Princeton had as "many as fifteen stages together starting from his house each way at the same time. A hundred horses would stand waiting to take the place of the wearied ones as they arrived," according to John F. Hageman.

The Bayleses and the Gulicks of the Kingston area ran the Union Line of stages.

During the first quarter of the nineteenth century corporations were formed to build the turnpike toll roads, such as the New Brunswick Pike (now Route 1), and the Princeton Pike (from Trenton via Mercer Street in Princeton, out Route 27 to Kingston, and then over Raymond Road to join the New Brunswick Pike).

Nineteenth-century engraving of an 1818
stagecoach

Main Street (once the Assunpink Trail) in Kingston, about 1970. Phineas Withington, who arrived at the village in 1810, ran the famous Union Line Hotel, which burned in 1889. It was replaced by the building at the right, also called the Union Line Hotel

In 1796, William Wintherbotham, an English traveller, suggested routes for a cross-Jersey canal, but he was little heeded by the stage and road companies or the busy inn-keepers. One of his routes followed the Raritan and Millstone rivers and then went down the Assunpink into the Delaware. The idea of such a canal was prevalent enough for Morse to mention it in his *Geography* of the same year. Then during the first quarter of the nineteenth century a series of plans, committees and companies centered upon the prospect of a canal. William Paterson (Governor from 1791–94) was among the promoters in 1804. The most spectacular proposal (from map-maker Christopher Colles, who was also an engineer) was for a timber aqueduct, high over the Jersey landscape.

Obviously a shipway cannot have waterfalls, and the rolling central Jersey countryside presented difficulties for a direct route between the Delaware and the Raritan. To overcome elevations, canals had to be devised with schemes such as locks to raise or lower vessels to another plane and provide a nearly level waterway.

Rutgers
University
Press

A review copy from

PASSAGE BETWEEN RIVERS:
A Portfolio of Photographs
with a History of the Delaware
and Raritan Canal
   by Elizabeth G. C. Menzies

Cloth, $9.50   Paper, $4.95

May we have two copies of your review?

30 COLLEGE AVENUE, NEW BRUNSWICK, N. J. 08901

Canals competed with road transportation. Note the boat in the lock in the background

The canal at East Millstone. The dock, at left, once extended into the present green

26

The Delaware and Raritan Canal Company, chartered in 1824 to James Neilson of New Brunswick and three others, hoped to build what was estimated as an $800,000 waterway. But the charter included a clause requiring the consent of Pennsylvania before June 1826 to the use of a feeder canal to take water from the Delaware River. Too many Philadelphia businessmen feared that money, rather than water, would be diverted to New Jersey. Some believed that a canal would "make N York the importers for Phil[a]," volunteered a merchant conversing on a stagecoach with John Pintard.

According to Daniel Webster, a friend of the famous lawyer Richard Stockton (son of the "Signer," and a non-stockholding "manager" of the company), the charter had so clearly become void in 1826 that the matter was hardly worth a legal opinion.

Neilson tried again, but the new Act of Incorporation was passed by the Legislature on February 4, 1830, the very same day as the Act for the Camden and Amboy Railroad.

The Camden and Amboy "Dinky" (the local name for the branch train to Princeton) at Princeton Junction after 1864, when the railroad tracks along the canal were taken up and the line straightened between Trenton and Monmouth Junction. This became the great Pennsylvania main line and is now called ConRail. (Princeton University Library photograph)

When the feeder canal was finally built, it carried traffic as well as water from the Delaware River. In the cold winter months, however, both the feeder and the main channel froze and were not usable for ship traffic. Often the canal was drained and repaired in this season. The controversy about water from the Delaware was dropped, because Pennsylvania also wanted to use the water—for the Delaware Division Canal.

A booster water supply, obtained by building a dam across the Raritan near Bound Brook, not only maintained the channel water level, but provided the power to turn mills at New Brunswick

The long monopoly of the stage and innkeeping business was about to be broken, but the new types of transportation would lead to another monopoly. The stages had been charging the high fee of six dollars for the all-day run between Philadelphia and New York, and innkeepers had had travellers at their mercy by also charging high fees and providing minimal service.

The two rival stage lines could not agree in their efforts to block new transportation. The Union Line supported the railroad, but lobbied against the canal, while the Peoples' Line took the opposite view, supporting the canal and resisting the railroad.

The Canal Company, nervous about the railroad, put its stock up for sale a week before the Camden and Amboy did. But then the railroad sold its entire issue of stock in ten minutes.

The Canal Company charter would have been void again if it had not sold its stock within a year. On April 6 (1830) Robert Field Stockton, Richard Stockton's second son and a Navy officer, borrowed from his wealthy father-in-law, John Potter, and saved the day by buying 4,800 shares. He became president of the company, his brother-in-law, John Renshaw Thomson, secretary, and James Neilson, treasurer.

Railroad, canal, and stagecoach of the nineteenth century

At East Millstone, the old Franklin Inn (built ca. 1734) now houses an antique shop and canoe rental. Unlike most inns it was helped by the canal upon whose bank it stands. (Picture taken in 1975)

Robert Stockton managed to meet two of the three Stevens brothers (Robert L. and John C.) at a New York theater, where, with his forceful, energetic, and charming personality, he persuaded them to join the Railroad Company with the Canal Company. The "Marriage Act" was passed by the Legislature on February 15, 1831. The State then passed an act, on March 2, entitling it to receive $30,000 a year plus percentages of freight and passenger fees from the Joint Companies. The legislators included a clause to prohibit the building of competitive transport routes across the waist of New Jersey for the thirty-year life of the charter (extended to fifty years). Thus, competition was precluded and staging became obsolete. The Conestoga freight wagons fell into disrepair.

The railroad through Bordentown, Hightstown, and Spotswood to South Amboy was completed at the end of 1832, and by 1839 a branch line ran along the canal through Princeton Basin to Kingston.

Robert Field Stockton, "engraved by H. B. Hall from a painting on ivory by Newton, London, 1840." Presumably this was Sir William John Newton (1785–1869), a London miniaturist, who became very popular, obtaining royalty, members of Parliament and of the aristocracy as subjects for his portraits

The more westerly of the two Princeton canal basins was filled in 1964 with the remains of the demolished University Art Museum (designed by A. Page Brown). Some of the molded Tiffany brick (from the Excelsior terra cotta and brick works in Perth Amboy) is visible in the foreground

The old "Coal Basin" still remains on the east side of Alexander Street, Princeton. The basins served as unloading docks and a place for overnight layovers. Small drawbridges allowed barges to pass through the basin-necks, which cut through the towpath

In 1830, Canvass White, a veteran canal engineer, and his associates (including Ashbel Welch, Jr., of Lambertville) made the survey for the canal—up the floodplains of the Raritan, Millstone, and Stony Brook rivers, across the 56- to 57-foot elevation to Trenton, and down the edge of the Delaware to Bordentown, the outlet. The estimated cost had risen from $800,000 to $1,175,000 (the railroad estimate was only $275,000). When completed the canal cost-overrun amounted to $1,655,000. The original stock issue was not enough to cover this enormous cost. As a financial crisis in America prevented borrowing at home, Robert Stockton, armed with his reassuring, persuasive manner, travelled to Europe and directly approached wealthy capitalists with remarkable success. Again he rescued the canal.

With much fanfare ground had been broken for the canal at the mid-point, Kingston, in November, 1830, before the "Marriage Act." In spite of an epidemic of cholera, prevalent in both Europe and among the Irish canal laborers in 1832, the level stretch from Kingston to Trenton was useable in the fall of 1833. As the canal neared completion, Canvass White died, and Ashbel Welch replaced him as chief engineer. On June 25, 1834, Governor Vroom triumphantly· opened the canal with a run in borrowed barges through the feeder canal, and next day through the entire length of the forty-three-mile main channel from Bordentown to New Brunswick.

At New Brunswick, a two-masted schooner sails in the canal, while two horsemen tow a barge. Usually mules were employed in towing, and the driver might sit on the rear mule, or "shafter"

A narrow pass-through for ropes. On the left is a pillar supporting the Princeton "Dinky" bridge

The canal had been more difficult to build than the railroad. It needed over 60 pivot bridges, 14 locks with centrally pivoted shutter sluices, an extra lift lock at Lambertville for the narrower 21½-mile feeder canal, also a guard lock at Raven Rock and one at Stockton, aqueducts, houses for the keepers and mule drivers, and stables for the animals. Dams had to be built on the Delaware and the Raritan to supply water for the canal.

Further expense resulted from the length of the route with its extra fifteen-mile dog-leg down the Millstone to avoid difficult elevations. However the engineers were successful in being permitted to enlarge the dimensions to 75 feet at the water-line, 60 feet across the bottom, and 8 feet deep. This allowed deep-keeled sloops and schooners to be towed through. The feeder was only 60 feet at the waterline. The locks were only 24 feet wide and 110 feet long (lengthened to 220 feet at mid-century). Yet greater barges could pass through than in the earlier Morris Canal from Phillipsburg to Jersey City, with its 75-foot-long by 9-foot-wide locks, and the D. & R. thus took the Lehigh coal trade away from the Morris. In addition, however, the D. & R. resorted to cutthroat monetary competition.

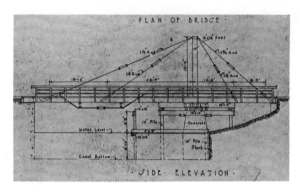

Kingston swing bridge
(scale drawing by W.P.A. about 1940)

Before 1858, the channel had been narrowed at bridge crossings to allow a shorter bridge span. As canal traffic grew, the waterway was widened to 48 feet at bridges to allow boats to pass each other. All but two bridges had to be correspondingly lengthened. There are several old pictures of A-frame swing bridges (see page 49), one of which carried Route 27 traffic at Kingston, but in the early 1900s the neater, less cumbersome king-post variety was installed there. This type was so well balanced that it could be opened by a man or woman (some of the bridge-tenders were women) pushing hard against one end, after disengaging the fastening to the roadway

Detail of the Princeton "Dinky" swing bridge

The sheer-leg, A-frame swing bridges relied on chains stretching under the canal to open and close them. When open the bridges paralleled the canal. A heavy-timbered framework protected them from boat damage when in this position. Iron bascule bridges were installed in later years at important Trenton streets. Originally 37 bridges crossed the feeder canal and 29 crossed the main channel.

Of all those movable bridges only one remains, rollers wedged, as no masted vessel will again pass through. It is the railroad bridge (probably built in the 1890s) for the famed Princeton "Dinky." Once there was a wooden A-frame swing bridge there, but then a more substantial iron swing bridge had to be installed to accommodate the heavier trains. It rotated on a rusticated stone pillar (fashionably corresponding with contemporary architecture) with a fixed cog-wheel on top of it. Manpower turned a small cog attached to the bridge to swing it.

At left of the picture is the A-frame swing bridge, and behind it the old railroad station at Rocky Hill. Rockingham, Washington's Headquarters, is in its original position above Howell's Quarry. All is changed today. The horseman rides along the canal bank, which is faced with stone blocks, like a Dutch dyke. (State of New Jersey lithograph at Rockingham)

Former Princeton "Dinky" on the A-frame bridge of the Camden and Amboy Railroad. The pass-through to facilitate handling ropes is visible below the flatcar. (Princeton University Library photograph)

The present Princeton "Dinky" crossing the last remaining
swivel bridge on the canal

The canal houses, which were of two designs, did not conform to the Georgian fashion of their day but reverted to a more mediaeval and utilitarian plan. They were simple two-story affairs with a front window for each room, two above and two below (four windows on the façade).

Those of stone have lasted longer than the wooden clapboard type, which usually had a central chimney that helped conserve heat, as in the old New England houses. One of these remains at Port Mercer (once Port Windsor), an inland harbor village that arose after the canal.

Port Mercer and the wooden canal house with a central chimney. Here Quaker Road, which Washington took to surprise the British at Princeton (January 3, 1777), was altered to parallel the canal for a short distance

Stone canal house at the village of East Millstone, whose growth was only slightly stimulated by the canal but which expanded when the railroad to New Brunswick was built in 1855. (About 1975)

Blackwell's or Runyonstown has a Victorian bridge-keeper's hut with bay windows. (About 1975)

The stone canal houses, several of which are still extant between Kingston and South Bound Brook, usually had a chimney on either end with a bake oven protruding from the kitchen exterior wall. At Weston and Zarephath, the bake ovens still bulge from the chimney walls.

The Kingston canal house is typical with its asymmetrical front door opening to a stair that divides the main floor into two rooms, the smaller of which, though labelled "living room" in the W.P.A. drawing, was clearly not the lived-in room. The large kitchen, like the mediaeval hall or keep, with its big fireplace, was where the family lived, cooked and ate.

Southern View of Bound Brook.

W.P.A. measured drawings of the Kingston canal house

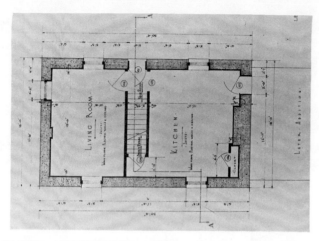

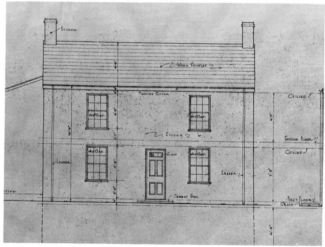

Bound Brook across the canal and the Raritan River. After following the floodplain of the Millstone from Aqueduct, the canal borders the Raritan from South Bound Brook to New Brunswick

Wild plum growing on the canal bank near Kingston. The Millstone River is beyond

Princeton Basin about 1872

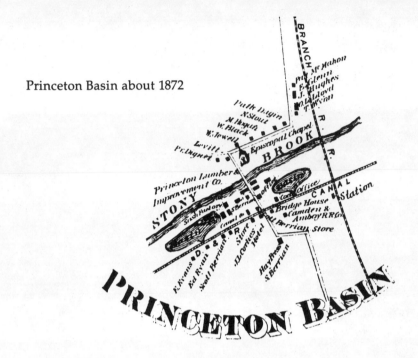

The main office of the Canal Company was at the Princeton Basin, giving it special importance. Robert F. Stockton built Canal Street (now Alexander Street) from Morven, the family mansion, along the edge of the first Stockton settlers' land (bought in 1696) to the Basin. In 1855, it was converted to a fashionable plank road (subject to rotting).

The basins at Kingston also attracted commercial buildings. The business district of the village began to shift from the top of the hill to the foot, beside the canal. A post office, stores, and a hotel appeared there.

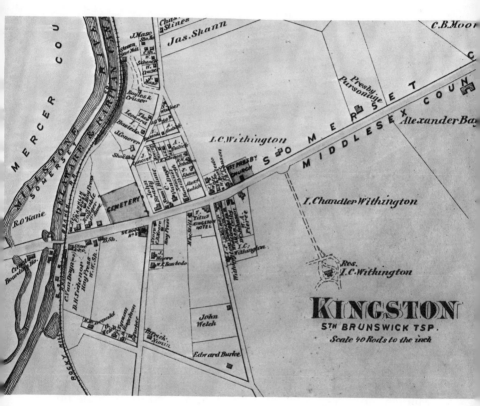

Kingston Lock, swing bridge, and basins with post office and shops. The old village lay to the right of the cemetery (where Washington turned toward Millstone). (Map from F. W. Beers's *State Atlas of New Jersey*, 1872, lent by Richard M. Stout)

61

Morven, on Stockton Street, Princeton, deeded to the State in 1954 and now the Governor's mansion, was built about 1758 by Richard Stockton, the signer of the Declaration of Independence. Robert F. Stockton, "the Commodore," president of the Joint Companies, moved from 1 Bayard Lane to Morven after the death (1827) of his father, Richard "the Duke" Stockton, Jr.

The canal barges excelled at transporting heavy building materials, and while the canal never made the profits the railroad did, it brought considerable income to the village of Princeton, where many of its officers resided. So many of the Stockton relatives were connected with the canal that it was almost a Stockton enterprise.

Though the need for a bank was recognized in 1827, the Princeton Bank was not incorporated until 1834, after the canal had been built. Among the corporators were John and William Gulick and Robert Bayles of the Kingston area, who ran the great Union Stage Line. The Crusers of Rocky Hill were also among the founders. Phineas Withington, then forty-four, the Kingston innkeeper and part owner of the Union Line, was not among the founders, presumably because he died that year. The families concerned with staging were now diversifying their interests in more productive enterprises at Princeton, the canal center.

The last of the lumber and building supply firms on Canal Street. In the 1930s there were three, and some sold coal as well. Their heavy products were well suited to barge transportation

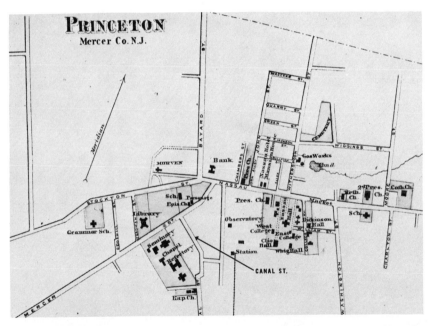

Map of Princeton in 1872, showing the head of Canal Street, Morven, and the Bank. (From F. W. Beers's *State Atlas of New Jersey*)

Lower Canal Street (now Alexander Street), near the basin, in the early 1960s

The first bank at Princeton was built near the head of Canal Street in 1836. Carpenter-architect Charles Steadman had already constructed two Stockton mansions, 2 Nassau Street (now 1 Bayard Lane), and Thomson Hall (demolished by the Princeton Theological Seminary in the early 1970s), an Episcopal church of Greek design and a replacement, also of Greek design, for the Presbyterian church, which had been destroyed by fire. He had also extensively renovated Morven. Foreseeing progress and prosperity at Princeton and given the ease with which building supplies could be acquired, all by means of the new canal, Steadman bought up the land on the canal side of Stockton Street. He built houses on speculation on north Canal Street, Mercer Street, Stockton Street and Steadman Street (now Library Place). He apparently had access to Classical Revival builders' books, such as William Pain's *Practical House Carpenter or Youth's Instructor* of 1794, from which he produced his version of the Greek Revival style, popular in America in the 1830s. He built and "owned more houses than any other man in Princeton," according to John F. Hageman's *History of Princeton.* Steadman was buried in the Princeton Cemetery in the summer of 1868.

Thomson Hall in July 1972, shortly before demolition. Robert Stockton's sister, Annis, and her husband, John Renshaw Thomson, secretary of the Canal Company, had Steadman build the house about 1826. The Ionic capitals were Greek (not Roman), epitomizing the country's admiration at the time for ancient Greek democracy. The mansard roof and probably the grand ballroom at the far end were the improvements of the second Mrs. Thomson in the 1870s

The Princeton Bank, built by Steadman at 4 Nassau Street, shortly after the canal was opened. Originally it displayed a four-column Doric porch hung with guttae under the corona. The wide steps were replaced in Victorian days and the façade much altered by a bay window and dormers, instead of the pediment. The place became a garage in the 1920s, where Essex Coaches and Chandlers and later Cadillacs and Oldsmobiles were sold

Upper Alexander Street (Canal Street), Princeton, in the 1960s, where Charles Steadman built a number of his Classical Revival dwellings with ornamental cornices, small porticos, and leaded ornamental fanlights. Though his tracts of land were close to the College and Theological Seminary, he saw that the canal side of Princeton would be the most advantageous area for extensive development

Concurrently with Steadman's classical additions to Princeton in the 1830s, other less ambitious architectural construction appeared. Rocky Hill mill owner William Cruser, who lived at Rockingham, "Washington's Headquarters at Rocky Hill," stage operator William Gulick, though he already owned real estate at Kingston, and lawyer James Sproat Green bought some land on the west side of Princeton's Witherspoon Street. Green's wife was Elizabeth Stockton, and he was a son of Ashbel Green, one-time president of Princeton College. Like so many of the Stockton connections, he had an interest in the Canal Company of which he was a director, receiving 12 per cent and later 10 per cent on his canal stocks.

Of the three villages, these businessmen clearly believed that Princeton was the coming town. Green, a staunch supporter of President Andrew Jackson (who dubbed him New Jersey district attorney), influenced the naming of the new streets that the trio built off Witherspoon. Jackson Street was demolished, in the 1960s, to make way for Avalon Place. Green Street was named for the Canal Company director, and Quarry was simply named for a former quarry. Inornate, functional houses lined these streets.

Only a few new houses appeared in the other canal villages, such as Kingston, where, on Laurel Avenue, one or two closely follow the canal house design. None of the villages along the canal expanded to the degree of Princeton, the center of canal management.

The rear of Rockingham faces Route 518. Now on its third site, it was moved in order to expand the quarry. It belonged to William Cruser's father, who probably added the original double balcony at the front, which once had a fine view of the Millstone River and the canal. (Picture taken in 1973)

Laurel Avenue, Kingston, in 1973

Green Street, Princeton, in the 1960s

Of the two nearby cities, Trenton was perhaps more affected by the Joint Companies than New Brunswick. The lumber and stone for the advanced new prison (finished 1836), where the cells could be warmed by "tubes of hot water" to 65° F. on the coldest days, was transported by the canal.

Pastor John William Yeomans wrote of the 1830s that there occurred an "awakening enterprise of their venerable city, and . . . the business of the place showed signs of revival. . . ."

In 1839, Charles Steadman was called in from Princeton to begin Trenton's fine Greek Revival brick First Presbyterian Church. Immediately thereafter, he was hired to build a $70,000 Mercer County Courthouse complex, which led to his building, in Yeomans' account, "the row of cottages beyond the canal, and some other handsome dwellings. . . ." One of these was for the New Jersey chief justice, Henry W. Green, who became the State's chancellor in 1860.

It was not until 1848 that John A. Roebling (builder of the Brooklyn Bridge) moved his wire mill from Pennsylvania to Trenton. Trenton's greatest expansion occurred much later, between 1880 and 1920, when cheap foreign labor poured in.

The State Prison at Trenton with the canal and the "prison lock"

The Mercer County buildings (now replaced) on south Broad Street

State Street with a wagon passing the Presbyterian Church

Three engravings published in 1844

The First Presbyterian Church of Trenton in 1976. Though much of Trenton's manufacturing developed in the second half of the nineteenth century, there had been an earlier period promoted by the completion in 1834 of the Delaware Falls Company's wing dam at Scudder's Falls, with a race to carry the water to turn the mills in the city. The prosperity brought by the mill race and the canal is reflected in the elegance of this fine Church. The Greek Revival design by Charles Steadman displays an *in antis* façade with massive free-standing Greek Ionic columns and capitals supporting the pediment. The crowning tower displays the Corinthian order, and once had a second tier; the combination of the two orders in this manner is reminiscent of the work of Sir James Gibbs. However, Steadman probably based his design (already tried out at Princeton) in large part on Asher Benjamin's *American Builder's Companion*. In its original form this church ranked among Steadman's best works. It is unfortunate that the tower's second tier has been replaced by an inverted aluminum ice-cream cone, but the craftsmanship for the intricate wood-carving of the Corinthian capitals was perhaps not available when repairs were required in recent times. (The top of the steeple, weakened by the 1955 hurricane, had to be dismantled in 1956. The replacement appeared in 1964.)

Robert Stockton returned to the navy (from 1838 to 1850) and at once obtained leave to study naval design improvements in Britain, where he met the Swedish engineer, John Ericsson. The enthusiastic Stockton ordered, at his own expense, two screw-propelled tugs of Ericsson's design. Only one was built: the *Robert F. Stockton,* which crossed the Atlantic in 1839, and became the first iron-hulled, screw-propelled vessel to come to the United States. Captain Crane, four men (one of whom was lost overboard) and a boy brought her over in forty-six days under sail alone. The *Great Britain* is usually called the first screw-propelled iron vessel to cross the Atlantic. She came much later (1845), taking less than fifteen days, but she came under steam. The *Robert F. Stockton,* registered here as the *New Jersey* (1840), brought about the age of steam tugs in American canals and was the prototype for the warship *Princeton.*

Stockton, at about the same time, raised British money for the Joint Companies, and with it purchased controlling shares in the Delaware Bridge Company and the Philadelphia and Trenton Railroad, which had planned to circumvent the previously mentioned monopoly law by building a track along the already existing New Brunswick Pike, which, to protect themselves, the Joint Companies also purchased. Only then was the Philadelphia and Trenton Railroad permitted to build a line (always referred to as the Camden and Amboy) running from Trenton along the canal through Princeton Basin to Kingston (finished January, 1839), then on by Monmouth Junction to New Brunswick (finished 1840).

In 1864, the Camden and Amboy straightened its track between Trenton and Monmouth Junction, and took up the rails beside the canal for use elsewhere.

An 1880 engraving (detail) showing a steam lighter in the canal at New Brunswick. Neilson and Stockton started a print cloth factory here about 1845. In the mid-century, rubber companies were built at a number of points along the canal: three plants at New Brunswick. A wallpaper firm also chose a canal-side location there, as did a sawmill in the 1860s and a fruit-canning plant in the 1880s

Nineteenth-century engraving of the thirty-ton *Robert F. Stockton* making her crossing of the Atlantic (1839). The 70-ft.-×-10-ft. vessel drew three feet and was powered by a 50-horsepower two-cylinder steam engine. Still in use in 1866, she was soon afterwards thoroughly

destroyed by Messrs. Stevens of Hoboken, following a request from the British Patent Office Museum to Ericsson for her engines. He thought the Messrs. Stevens acted thus to protect their image as the originators of screw propulsion in 1804. However, John Fitch had already applied a screw or worm propeller to a small steamboat in 1796

Early railroad cars resembled horse carriages, and indeed the Camden and Amboy used horses to draw its first trains. In 1840, it boasted two open flatcars with rocking chairs for its more restless passengers

The last remaining stretch of the old Camden and Amboy Railroad in the area, between Kingston and the present ConRail main line at Deans Pond, now Monmouth Junction. It is used solely by the trap rock quarry at Kingston today. (Picture taken in the late 1960s)

The wake of the steam vessels eroded the canal banks; therefore a rip rap, or stone facing, had to be built and a speed limit of four and a half miles an hour imposed. A telegraph system served as a speed check and to warn lock keepers to prepare their locks in time for oncoming boats.

The steam packet boat service remained minimal with its peak of 136 passengers, mostly out for pleasure, in 1849. For many years the 208-foot freight steamers of the Baltimore Line passed through the canal daily. (The "new and splendid" passenger barge, *New Jersey,* advertised in 1834, had been too slow.)

In spite of steam, mules (cheaper), hitched in tandem, hauled much of the barge traffic. Princeton canal stockholder, Richard S. Conover, owned a string of barges requiring 300 four-mule teams. The Montana mules, broken at the canal by "muleskinners," did a fourteen-mile stint a day. Changes of mules were available at points along the waterway. Some of the barges and steamboats were built at Lambertville on the feeder canal; steamers were also built at Shurt's yard in South Bound Brook, but they received a setback when their vessel the *Molison* blew up at Five Mile Lock.

Transport was concentrated on the coal trade. Anthracite, once thought unburnable and only good for road metal, came from the Mauch Chunk mines in Pennsylvania. The 90-by-10-foot-beam coal barges, often of the "squeezer," or divisible "hinge" type, were called "Chunkers," from Mauch Chunk. Those bringing coal from the Schuylkill Fields, near Pottstown, by the Schuylkill Navigation Canal were the "Skukers," and were towed up the Delaware to the Bordentown Lock.

A steam passenger vessel in the canal near the Albany Street Bridge, New Brunswick, about 1880

Mules in tandem pulling a barge near Princeton. (Princeton University Library photograph.)

Mules were always cheaper than steam, and especially large mule stables were maintained at the entrances to the canal. Bordentown boasted stables for 200 teams to accommodate the heavy barge traffic that sometimes reached 115 barges in a single day

The outlet lock at Lambertville in 1963: the "Chunkers" came down the Lehigh and Delaware Division canals, at first to Bristol, and later, after the exit lock was built, only to New Hope, where they crossed the Delaware by hitching, partially broadside on, to a pulley on a wire across the river to Lambertville, where an outlet lock for the feeder had been built about 1840; then the current supplied the pressure to move them along the wire

The Lehigh Navigation canal at Mauch Chunk, before 1843

85

A last remnant of the once prosperous Princeton Basin in 1975: here stands the building of the Railroad Hotel (later the Union Hotel) from the days of the Camden and Amboy Railroad. Mule stables stood behind it, and next it Scott Berrien's store of the 1870s offered "silk waists, kid gloves, evening gowns, curtains, dressing sacks, blankets, candles, wax, Mrs. Mary Brown's chewing tobacco, tow lines." What more could anyone want?

Coal was the real mainstay of canal transport. The canal served as a conveyor between the flanking states of Pennsylvania and New York rather than as an extensive developer of New Jersey itself.

Perhaps the most notable of the building cargoes were the slabs and ornament of terra cotta, molded and baked at the Rocky Hill works of the Atlantic Terra Cotta Company and sent by canal to New York to cover the great Woolworth Building (tallest of its day) in 1913. (It has recently come to light that some of the ornament was produced at Atlantic's Perth Amboy plant.)

As they passed through the farm areas of Central New Jersey, the canal-boats picked up some agricultural cargoes. Within living memory, Cortelyou's apples, gathered in Franklin Township near Rocky Hill, were shipped to the New Brunswick market by barge. Persons in Hunterdon County were eager to distribute their produce by the feeder and in 1831 obtained a charter for a railroad to lead to the canal near Lambertville, but the railroad itself did not materialize for some time.

The strip mines at the summit of Mauch Chunk mountain. (Engravings published in 1843)

The canal near Griggstown

The Canal Company moved its offices from the Princeton Basin closer to the aging management in town. Lawyer Richard Stockton Field, a shareholder, had built a law school (ca. 1848) connected with Princeton College, but it lasted only for a short time. After 1855, the Canal Company used the brownstone Gothic building situated on Mercer Street at the top of Canal Street. It had been designed by John Notman of Philadelphia, whom the Stockton connections had brought in to build elegant Tuscan villas in the new Italianate style.

The investors in the Canal Company had been receiving a steady 10 per cent on their stocks for over three decades. Many of the Stockton relatives were, as well as shareholders, prominent lawyers and politicians, serving to promote the welfare of the Joint Companies at high levels. Their extensive wealth did much to improve Princeton's architecture over that of nearby villages. Had there not been the sea-faring Robert Stockton to build a shipping lane through his inland home-town and gather his clan to promote it, Princeton might have grown up differently. Then perhaps Kingston might with its coaching and its inn business have become a more prominent town. Phineas Withington's son Isaac Chandler Withington, after some peregrinations and marrying well, also built an Italianate villa at Kingston in 1857, but his interests were in New York, not Kingston, which developed into a typical New Jersey workingman's town.

The small Gothic-cottage-style canal office by John Notman at 43 Mercer Street, Princeton, in the 1960s. It cost R. S. Field about $5,000

Isaac Chandler Withington's Italianate summer villa (1857) at Kingston

Prospect about 1964, designed by John Notman in 1849 for Thomas F. Potter (Robert Stockton's brother-in-law). "No one had more to do with stimulating interest in Italian architecture than John Notman, the young Scot who had settled in Philadelphia in 1831," says George Tatum in *Penn's Great Town*. In January 1848, Notman went to Princeton to discuss plans for an Italian-style mansion with the John Potter Stocktons to whom their father Robert Stockton gave the house. John was a lawyer for the Camden and Amboy Railroad, and later, when he was appointed minister to the Papal State, he sold the house back to his father. It stands at 83 Stockton Street and is now called Lowrie House. Notman built still a third Tuscan villa for Richard Stockton Field (called Fieldwood and then Guernsey Hall). He also renovated the Princeton College building, Nassau Hall, after the 1855 fire, adding Italian stair towers to either end (since partially removed), and designed a number of other Princeton buildings, including a rural gothic farmhouse for Robert Stockton's son Richard, who became secretary and treasurer of the Camden and Amboy Railroad.

Prospect was turned over to Princeton College, later Princeton University, after Thomas Potter's death in 1877, and housed their presidents until the 1960s, when it was turned into a faculty club and the John Potter Stockton villa, which the University received, became the president's mansion

Changes came as the original management of the Companies aged.

James Neilson, the Canal Company treasurer and early initiator of the canal, a veteran of the war of 1812, died at age 78.

The ebullient and dynamic Commodore Robert Stockton died at age 71 in 1866, the canal's most prosperous year, and was replaced as president of the Canal Company by his third son, Robert, who was also secretary and treasurer of Ashbel Welch's Belvidere and Delaware Railroad. As the Stockton dynasty continued, Bayard Stockton, son of the Commodore's son Richard, became president.

Edwin Augustus Stevens of the railway outlived his brother Robert by twelve years. He was treasurer of the Camden and Amboy and general manager of the Joint Companies, but he died in Paris in 1868, leaving money for the noted Stevens Institute of Technology (chartered 1870) in his home town of Hoboken. His granddaughter, Congressional Representative Millicent Fenwick, now has part of the canal district in her care.

The Stevens Institute of Technology, Hoboken. (From an engraving of ca. 1890)

A milestone on the towpath. Placed at an easily visible angle, one side gave the mileage to New Brunswick and the other to Bordentown

Ashbel Welch, engineer-builder of the Delaware and Raritan Canal, recipient of an honorary A. M. from the College of New Jersey at Princeton (1843), builder and president of the Belvidere and Delaware Railroad, inventor of the American railroad signal system (1863), and vice-president of the Camden and Amboy from 1862 to 1867, became the executive officer of the Joint Companies. At the beginning of 1867 he effected the consolidation with the New Jersey Railroad and Transportation Company to gain its track from New Brunswick to the Hudson River with the ferry rights. The combine became the Associated Companies and then the United Companies. The same year, the Honorable John M. Read charged, he purchased, "without knowledge of the stockholders," a strip of land that eventually became the Hudson Terminal. He then headed the United Companies as the General President as well as the Chief Engineer. But his expansion policies used up the Companies' capital, which had been invested at 6 per cent and contributed to the high dividends that had continued over so many years. Though the coal tonnage of the canal was greater than ever before, rising from 540,000 tons in 1847, to 2,326,000 tons in 1871, the dividends of all the Companies in 1870 suddenly fell below the long established 10 percent.

Ashbel Welch (from an engraving of about 1880) was born in Madison, N. Y., in 1809, but resided in Lambertville by 1832, when he engineered the feeder canal and then the main channel (after the death of Canvass White). When he lengthened the locks in the winter of 1852, he used 4,000 men to finish the job in three months, while keeping within his cost estimate. By inventive methods of housing and heating the new concrete, he ingeniously prevented it from freezing as it set

Behind the rubber works at Lambertville (ca. 1880) three mules pull a barge on the feeder canal. The train from the Belvidere and Delaware Railroad had become part of the Pennsylvania Railroad. The Delaware River and New Hope are in the background

The feeder canal at a point between Trenton and Scudder's Falls: the open water flows through Trenton to the Freeway, where the main channel has been covered over. (The section in the city south of the feeder-junction has been filled in.) Though the ice here looks tempting enough to skate on, canals are a hazard to skaters because of the slow but steady current washing away the ice from below. Fluctuations in water level may also cause a crust of ice to become dangerously unsupported

Their pocketbooks suddenly shrunk, the directors (one of whom was John Jacob Astor, with 100 shares of Canal stock) met in 1871. They heard from the chief Canal Company stockholder, John M. Read (470 shares), the lawyer who had early on settled a dispute over Delaware River water for the canal, and defended the railroad in "suits and claims . . . growing out of the terrible accident near Burlington." He proclaimed that the Companies should accept the offer of a 999-year lease from the Pennsylvania Railroad. It saw Welch's acquisitions as major assets and was prepared to guarantee 10 per cent dividends to all the United Companies stockholders. Read approved of the late Edwin Stevens' management, but strongly disapproved of the handling by Welch, under whose guidance the dividends had fallen through dependence on profits alone. He emphatically finished his diatribe against Welch's management with, "ONE THING IS CERTAIN, OUR OFFICIAL HEAD, THE GENERAL PRESIDENT, MUST NOT BE AN ENGINEER." He had already (in 1869) condemned Welch, a builder (under his brother) of the Lehigh Canal and a director of the Lehigh Coal and Navigation Company, for approving certain decisions of that company after a disastrous flood that cut off the Mauch Chunk coal. Read maintained that to make the Chief Engineer also the General President "made him really the judge of his own plans and expenditures," and that the engineer should only be "the subordinate of the president."

The directors resolved to remove Welch as General President and separate the office of Chief Engineer and to accept the Pennsylvania's lease.

ON THE DELAWARE.

Delaware River. (From Coffin's *Old Times in the Colonies*, 1881)

105

The towpath in the 1970s: no mule-barge could pass here today with those nearby fifty-year-old trees lining the canal bank. Growth on the berm-bank (opposite the towpath) would matter less. Mules towing in either direction used the same tow path. If two barges met, one could pass her lines over the other; alternatively, the lines could be unhitched and thrown aboard the vessel momentarily. More often the downstream barge would slow its mules, pull over toward the berm-bank, and drop its slack hawsers under the oncoming Trenton-bound barge. The trees serve in this present period of the canal's history as an attractive habitat for many of the over 150 species of birds that reside in New Jersey. The nearby water is an extra enticement for them

In 1869, the Legislature had lowered the rail rate of coal to two cents a ton-mile, a blow to the canal. In spite of all, the canal's net earnings were $706,779 in 1873.

The monopoly of the Joint Companies had been extended in 1854, but expired at the end of 1868. The 1870s were a chaotic period, with railroads vying for possession of the freight. The Reading Railroad built its major line across the State in 1876, taking the Mauch Chunk coal trade. Spurred by this competition, the Pennsylvania in 1893 enlarged its line through Princeton Junction into a main four-track railroad. The canal was left to carry less and less.

By 1922 other goods (150,000 tons) exceeded the older most important cargo, coal (75,000 tons), by a wide margin. Oil was the new fuel.

Small, empty mule-towed barge about 1918. (Photograph by
Alan W. C. Menzies)

The approach to the Griggstown Lock in 1975

The canal metamorphosed into a conveyance for gentlemen's yachts; some taking the inland waterway to Florida. The demanding toots resounded from afar, as the cruisers blew for the opening of bridges and locks. If the lock gate had been opened in time all went well, otherwise the yacht lost steerageway and might be blown broadside across the canal or into the bank. As the slow-moving gates were levered open by the keeper's steady push against the long wooden bar (once the gates had been mechanized), the oncoming vessel threw her engines into reverse as a brake. The shore-hand jumped to the bank to catch the stern-rope first, as the vessel slackened to a halt within the lock. The thrower had divided his light rope into two coils and followed through with his lefthand coil. The shore-hand hauled it in fast to quickly grab the loop on the attached hauser and snub it over the bollard, or snubbing post as it was called on the D. and R. The bow-rope always came second, then the yacht sat bound and waiting for the snail-paced gates to close and the shutter-sluices to open to let the water in or out to raise or lower the vessel to the next level of the canal. On a fine day, it was pleasant work, but the canal could not subsist on this.

A gentleman's yacht near St. Joseph's College, in 1918. (Photograph by Alan W. C. Menzies)

A modern-day cruise on the canal near the Princeton Basin

After functioning for a century, the canal, which had not made a profit since 1900, closed its gates to navigation in the depression year of 1933. (The feeder canal had already been closed since 1913.) Plants, such as the Atlantic Terra Cotta Company at Rocky Hill, were phased out. The unusual new angular drawbridge, built in 1931 for the expanding traffic on Route 1, was no longer raised. (It needed 110-foot girders to span a narrow 28-foot-wide section of the canal at Baker's Basin.) Between 1932 and 1934, the Pennsylvania Railroad Company negotiated a transfer of the canal to the State. Fortunately, the new owners began selling canal water to nearby industries, which perhaps saved the canal from being drained like the Morris Canal.

In the next few years the State and Federal governments considered a great ship canal to utilize the canal right of way. The plan would have deepened the Delaware River to Trenton. But the second World War came, and the Army Corps of Engineers abandoned the idea in 1942.

Soon the canal right of way was spotted as a route for a freeway through Trenton, and that section of the canal is forever lost.

In 1944 the State began replacing the old wooden lock gates by concrete dams with sluice gates to adjust water flow.

Willows reflected in the canal near Griggstown

The Penn-Central main line in early 1976, formerly the Pennsylvania Railroad, at Trenton, now part of ConRail

The lock at Kingston in the 1960s, without the old wooden gates, which were replaced by concrete dams with water-controlling sluices in 1944

As the drought of the early 1960s dried up the supply of drinking water, the State allowed water companies to pump from the canal into their filtering facilities. Towns such as Princeton bolstered their artesian well water with canal water. With the town's increasing population, the canal inevitably became a necessary water resource. New Brunswick now takes much more than half its water supply from the canal. But over the years, the canal has been silting up and growing shallower. The Bureau of Water Facility Operations, Division of Water Resources of the New Jersey Department of Environmental Protection, in charge of the water, had hoped to dredge the canal, using money from the 1975 water-bond issue, but the money-conscious voters of a recession year turned that bond issue (and a number of others) down.

As a supplier of drinking water, the canal must not be polluted by highway de-icers, oil, or other residues and debris. In the 1950s, the State ordered some of the leaking cesspools and emptying sewers along the waterway cleaned up. Bathing is specifically forbidden, especially within 300 feet of the North Brunswick Water Treatment Plant, which has a sign to this effect.

Fire hydrants are an accepted safety feature of towns and cities today. These, stored at Princeton, may some day spout canal water

The canal near the Princeton Basin in 1975

During the construction boom that produced great housing developments and shopping centers, it became clear that without planning the New Jersey landscape would be irrevocably altered for the worse, and many historic places lost for all time.

By the 1960s Margaret D. Woodring, a Rutgers University specialist in environmental design, had begun plans for a State park along the canal, using citizen participation in clearing the overgrown towpath. The Boy Scouts gave their help. The Canal Society of New Jersey was also an advocate of any measures that would preserve the canal and its intrinsic beauty.

When a new bridge was proposed in the late 1960s for the crossing of the Millstone River, at Kingston on Route 27, two nearby residents, Margen Penick and Charlotte Pierce, looked out sadly at the handsome, doomed eighteenth-century stone bridge. They were imaginative doers, not easily brushed aside by the Highway Department, and instead of the destruction of the fine old bridge, they proposed a small park about it with boat landings on the canal and the Millstone and a picnic grove. Commissioner Robert A. Roe and Parks Director Joseph Truncer officially approved the idea in January 1969, and by 1970 the park was in operation. Here was the nucleus for the Delaware and Raritan Canal State Park, suitably placed at the canal's point of initial construction.

Bureau of Parks sign at the Kingston Canal Park

View from the Canal Park showing the old stone bridge over the Millstone in 1971 with the former flour mill behind it

The Stony Brook-Millstone Watersheds Association launches canoes on the Millstone River in the Canal Park at Kingston. The route took them downstream on the fast-flowing Millstone to a portage point, where they returned via the relatively current-free canal

In spite of the official approval of a State park along the canal, the linear strip of land and water was constantly endangered by harmful encroachment in the late 1960s and early 1970s. Realizing this, Lee Bullitt and Margen Penick formed the Delaware and Raritan Canal Coalition to insure the preservation of the old waterway and its environs. The Coalition pressed for its designation as a historic site. Commissioner Richard J. Sullivan eventually declared it a State Historic Site in December 1972, and next year it achieved recognition as a National Historic Site, for many overlooked nineteenth-century structures are now being recognized as an indispensable part of our heritage. But this was not enough to insure preservation, so the State Legislature was approached. Senators Bateman and Schluter were instrumental in initiating a bill, which, among other things, set up a commission of eight with the Commissioner of Environmental Protection as a ninth member. The commission was empowered to prevent any detrimental construction that would harm the canal and to designate a green belt along it. On October 10, 1974, Governor Brendan Byrne signed that bill into law.

Such is the story of a waterway that has affected New Jersey, one way or another, for over 140 years. The Delaware and Raritan Canal has lived through a long and exciting past and a turbulent present. Its future offers a pleasant, healthy, natural recreation area and a life-giving water supply to the people of New Jersey.

An artist enjoys painting the flickering waters of the old canal

Leaves in the canal (a negative print)

CANAL, RIVER, & RAILROAD MAP

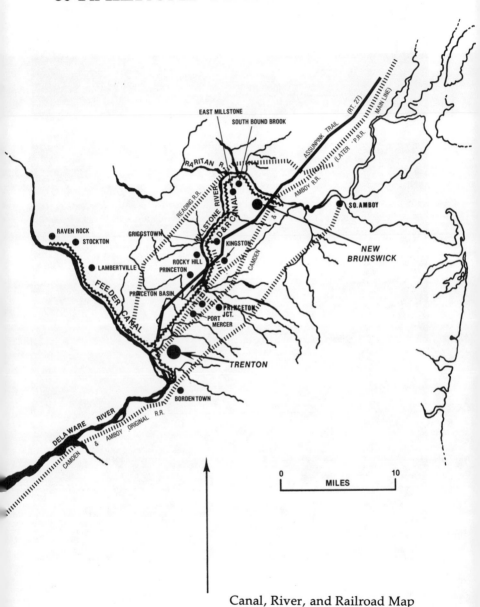

Canal, River, and Railroad Map